SCiENCE

Workbook

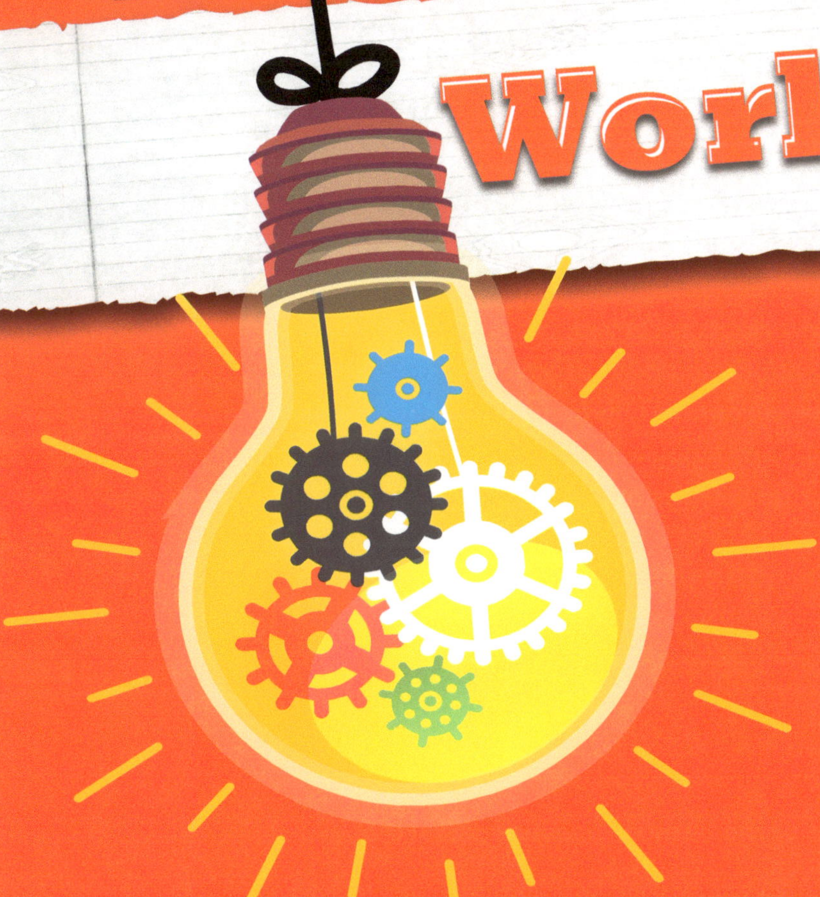

Level 2

Published in Moonstone
by Rupa Publications India Pvt. Ltd 2022
7/16, Ansari Road, Daryaganj
New Delhi 110002

Sales centres:
Allahabad Bengaluru Chennai
Hyderabad Jaipur Kathmandu
Kolkata Mumbai

ISBN: 978-93-5520-808-8

First impression 2022

10 9 8 7 6 5 4 3 2 1

Contents

Let's Revise 4

Plants. 9

World of Animals 13

Our Body 17

Food for Health 19

Safety Rules 21

House 23

Clothing 26

Air 28

Water 30

Day and Night 34

Test Yourself 1 36

Test Yourself 2 41

Answers 46

Let's Revise

A. Write the name of the animal which lives in the given home.

1. Hive

2. Burrow

3. Web

4. Nest

5. Stable

6. Shed

7. Pond

8. Kennel

9. Cave

10. Den

B. Read the statements given below and write T for true statements and F for false ones.

1. An ant is a big animal.

2. Crocodiles can live both on land and in water.

3. All living things need food to live.

4. Birds cannot live on land.

5. Soil is a non-living thing.

6. Plants take energy from animals.

C. Fill in the blanks with the correct words.

flower	climber	root	herb	seeds

1. A rose plant is a ___________________.

2. The plant of grapes is a ________________.

3. We eat the ______________ of a carrot plant.

4. New plants grow out of the ____________.

5. A ________________ changes into a fruit.

D. Name the sense organ you use for the following tasks.

1 

2

3

4 

5 

E. Answer the following questions in one sentence.

1. Why do we need food?

____

2. Why do we need a house?

____

3. Why do we wear clothes?

____

F. Name two rooms you have in your house.

G. Name two clothes you wear on a rainy day.

H. Name the following clothes?

I. **Can you tell how these types of houses are different from each other?**

Igloo　　　　　　Stilt House　　　　　　Log House

J. **Draw two man-made things in the space given below.**

Plants

There are various plants of different shapes and sizes all around us. Plants can be categorized as trees, shrubs, herbs, climbers and creepers. Plants are classified on the basis of the structure of their stem.

A. Read the names of the plants given in column I. Match them to the correct option in column II.

Column I	Column II
Watermelon	has seeds
Mint	has strong woody trunks
Banyan tree	is a herb
Tomato	is a creeper

B. Fill in the blanks with the correct words.

Help Box

land

Climbers

Herbs

Shrubs

tree

Creepers

water

1. A ______________ has a thick stem called trunk.

2. ______________ grow along the ground.

3. ______________ need support to climb up.

4. ______________ are very small plants which live for only for a few months.

5. Plants can grow both on ______________ and in ______________.

6. ______________ have thin and hard stems, they live for many years.

C. Answer the following questions.

1. Why do climbers and creepers need support to grow?

____

2. How are herbs different from shrubs?

____

3. Name three climbers:

____

4. Which types of plants live for many years?

____

5. What do plants need to make their food?

____

D. Name two plants which:

1. Grow in desert   ________________, ________________

2. Grow in water   ________________, ________________

3. Bear fruits   ________________, ________________

4. Bear vegetables   ________________, ________________

5. Bear flowers   ________________, ________________

6. Grow in soil   ________________, ________________

E. Name a plant which gives us:

1. Jute ___________________

2. Cotton fibre ___________________

3. Oil ___________________

4. Spices ___________________

F. Can you arrange the words from the help box in the order of a plant's growth?

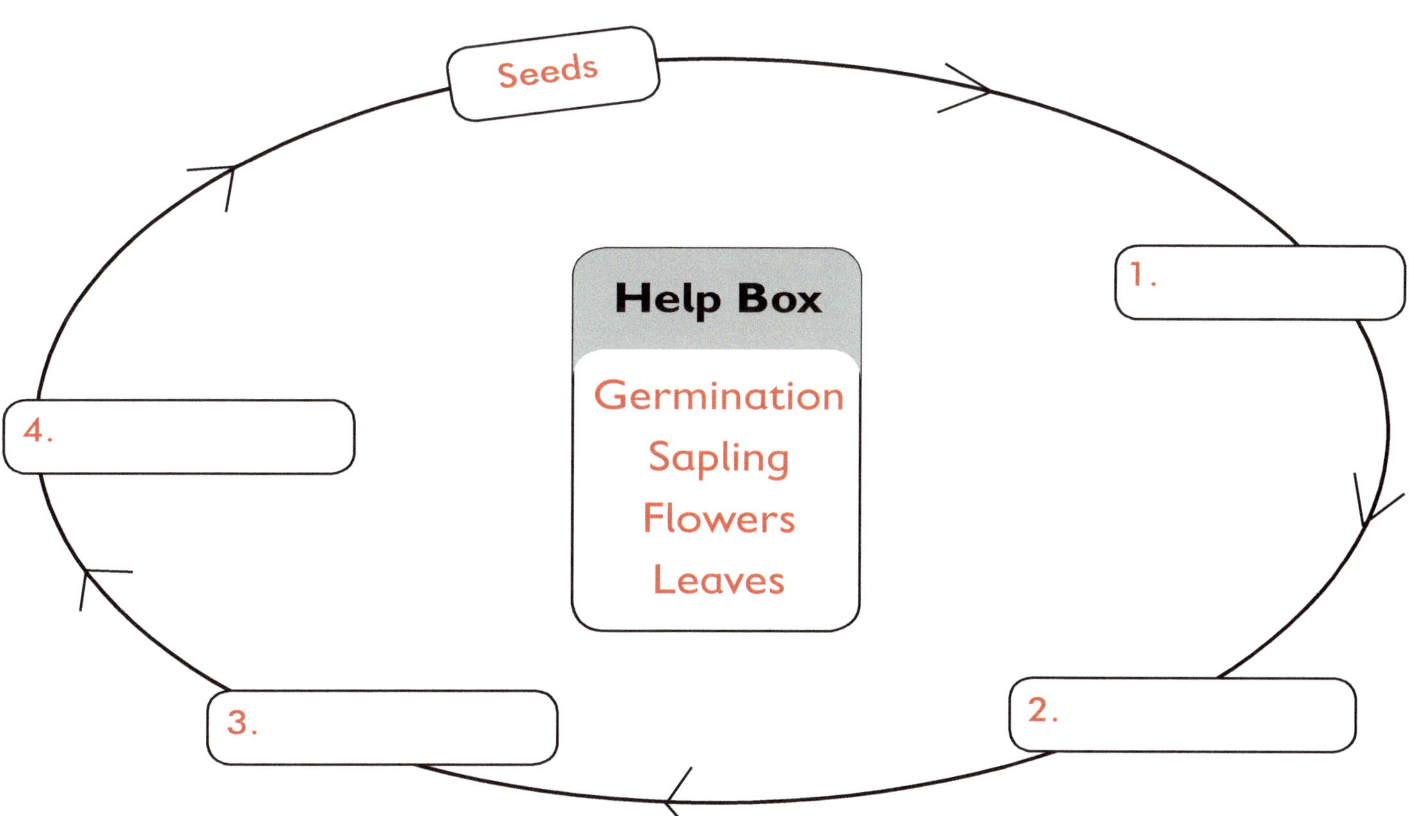

G. Six things that we get from plants are hidden in the word grid given below. All the six words start with the letter 'P'. Can you find them?

P	A	N	S	Y	C	R	I
B	E	D	P	P	M	O	P
J	Q	T	X	E	H	P	U
P	P	A	P	A	Y	A	L
U	E	G	Y	N	V	P	S
K	A	L	F	U	N	E	E
A	S	S	W	T	Z	R	S

____

____

____

____

____

____

____

H. Complete the concept map given below.

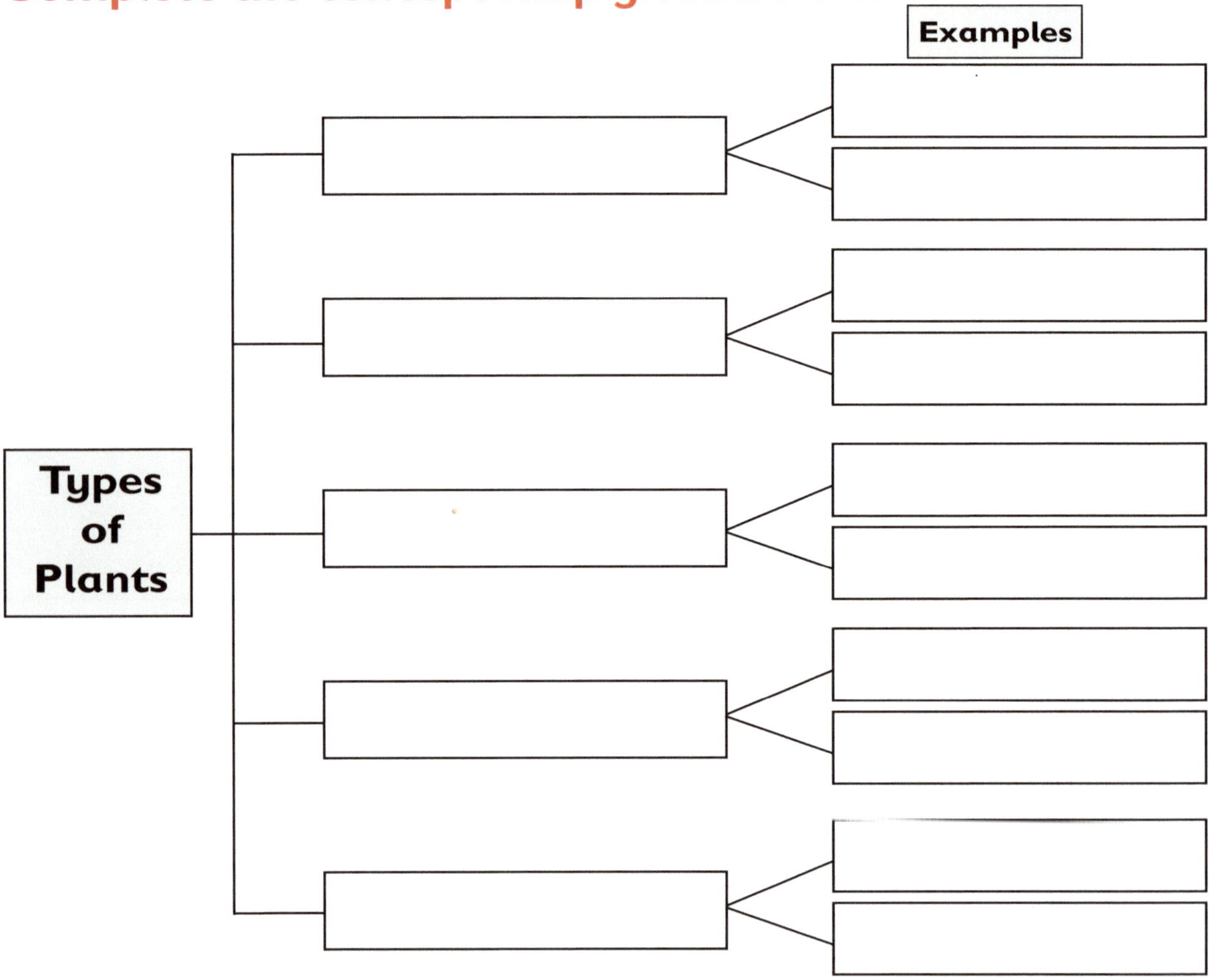

Types of Plants

World of Animals

Different animals have different features, habitats and food habits. Those which are kept at home or farm are called domestic animals while those which live in the forest are called wild animals and cannot be domesticated. Animals also need shelter to protect themselves and their babies from bad weather and other animals.

A. The names of some animals are listed below. Write 'D' for domestic animals and 'W' for wild animals.

1. Tiger

2. Leopard

3. Horse

4. Elephant

5. Sheep

6. Goat

7. Vulture

8. Camel

9. Bee

10. Giraffe

11. Rhinoceros

12. Duck

B. Match the animals with the products we get from them.

Column I	Column II
Sheep	Honey
Silkworm	Wool
Cow	Eggs
Hen	Silk
Bee	Milk

C. Write one word for the following.

1. A domestic animal which helps us move from one place to another.

    ____

2. An object which is used to make candle wax. _______________

3. A water animal which gives us eggs to eat. _______________

4. A worm which gives us silk. _______________

5. An animal which is kept to guard a farm or house. _______________

D. Name two animals which have:

1. Horns _______________, _______________

2. Tail _______________, _______________

3. Claws _______________, _______________

4. Wings   _____________________, _____________________

5. Shell   _____________________, _____________________

6. Mane   _____________________, _____________________

7. Hump   _____________________, _____________________

8. Stripes   _____________________, _____________________

9. Fur   _____________________, _____________________

10. Sting   _____________________, _____________________

E. Read the statements given below and choose the correct option.

1. An animal which is not a pet.

    Dog   Rabbit   Lion

2. An animal which is kept at farm.

    Snake   Duck   Hippopotamus

3. An animal that can live both on land and in water.

    Vulture   Zebra   Crocodile

4. An animal which eats other small animals.

    Hyena   Rhinoceros   Giraffe

1.   What are domestic animals?

____

2.   What are wild animals?

____

3.   Name three things we get from farm animals.

____

4.   Name two different places where animals live.

____

5.   Name three animals that carry heavy loads for us.

____

Our Body

Our body has many parts which perform specific functions. Some parts of our body are soft such as muscles and skin while the other parts are hard such as bones and teeth. Bones and muscles shape our body.

We should try to maintain a good posture. A straight and upright posture keeps our body in proper shape.

A. Name the body part which helps you to perform the activities given below.

1. See a photograph

2. Walk to school

3. Write your name

4. Smell a flower

5. Bite an apple

6. Kneel down for prayer

7. Bow your head

8. Smile for the camera

9. Listen to your teacher

10. Kick the football

B. Fill in the blanks with the correct words.

Help Box

206

joints

muscles

skeleton

posture

bones

exercise

1. Our body is made up of __________ and __________.

2. All the bones in the body together form the __________.

3. Our body has __________ bones.

4. We can bend our body at the __________.

5. Regular __________ keeps our muscles strong and fit.

6. The position in which we hold our body is called __________.

C. Find out whether the given statements are True (T) or False (F).

1. We should always sit with the back straight.

2. We should never sit upright.

3. We should exercise and play daily to stay healthy.

4. We should never lie down while reading.

5. The place where two bones meet is called a muscle.

6. The skull protects the brain.

7. Muscles cover the bones and help them to move.

8. Maintaining correct posture is not good for our body.

Food for Health

Food gives us energy and helps our body to grow. The food we eat can be divided into three major groups. These groups are energy-giving, body-building and protective food. One should eat different kinds of food items from each of these groups to stay healthy.

A. Name of some food items are given below. Find out the category each food item belongs to and fill the table accordingly.

Carrot	Wheat	Milk	Rice	Banana	Egg
Apple	Pulses	Meat	Potatoes	Orange	Beans
Grapes	Nuts	Yogurt	Tofu	Spinach	Oats

Protective food	Body-building food	Energy-giving food

B. Fill in the blanks with the correct word.

1. Eating _______________ food can make you sick. (fresh/stale)

2. We should wash our __________ before and after eating. (hair/hands)

3. Food gives us ________________ to work and play. (energy/time)

4. ________________________ foods make our muscles and bones strong. (Energy-giving/Body-building)

5. _______________ gives us energy to work. (Wheat/Milk)

6. We must drink plenty of ___________ to remain healthy. (water/soft drinks)

7. We should chew our ________________ well. (teeth/food)

8. Fruits and vegetables are called ____________________ foods. (protective/energy-giving)

C. Answer the questions given below.

1. Why do we need energy-giving foods?

   ____

2. Why do we need body-building foods?

   ____

3. What is a meal?

   ____

4. Why do we need protective food?

   ____

5. Why should we eat our meals at the right time?

   ____

Safety Rules

We should always observe the safety rules to avoid accidents. They also prevent us from getting hurt and should be followed at home, at school, in playground and on road.

Accidents can happen anywhere and anytime due to negligence.

A. **Read the statements given below and tick (✓) the actions which are safe to do.**

1. Follow the rules of the game you are playing. ☐

2. Open the door of a moving vehicle. ☐

3. Use sharp object without any supervision. ☐

4. Swimming in the presence of an adult. ☐

5. Take medicines on your own. ☐

6. Stay away from electrical equipments. ☐

7. Don't play on the roof or near the road. ☐

8. Move hands and head outside the window of a moving vehicle. ☐

B. Write one word for the following.

1. We should use it while crossing the road.

2. An object filled with air for kids who are learning to swim.

3. A signal device use to control the flow of traffic.

4. A device which gives out warning sound in case of emergency.

C. Cross out the objects which are unsafe to use in the box given below.

House

Our house protects us from bad weather, wild animals and other dangers. We build houses to suit our needs such as location, weather and family size. Some houses are temporary which can be moved from place to place while permanent houses are made of bricks and cement which cannot be moved to different places.

A. Rearrange the following letters to make a word related to house.

1. OORM ______________

2. FROO ______________

3. TTNE ______________

4. ODOR ______________

5. RIBKC ______________

6. TSNOE ______________

7. LFAT ______________

8. THU ______________

9. OOILG ______________

10. NETECM ______________

B. Choose the correct option for the following.

1. An igloo is made up of ______________ .

> mud   ice

2. A hut can be made using ______________.

> bricks and wood   mud and straw

3. A tent is made up of ______________ .

> cloth   stones

C. Read the names of different types of houses and categorise them as permanent or temporary.

Caravan	Bungalow	Apartment	Hut
Igloo	Tent	Cottage	Teepee
Castle	Flat	Mansion	Log cabin

Temporary Houses	Permanent Houses

D. Draw a teepee and a tent house. Discuss the differences and similarities between the two.

E. Fill in the blanks. Use the words from the clue box.

animals   temporary   house   roofs   weather   permanent

1. We need a ________________ to live in.

2. A house protects us from ____________ and bad ______________.

3. Houses made using cement, bricks and iron rods are called __________ house.

4. Tent, hut and caravan are examples of ________________ house.

5. Houses in the mountains have sloping ____________ .

F. Answer the following questions.

1. Two things used to make permanent houses.

   __________________________ and __________________________

2. Two things used to make temporary houses.

   __________________________ and __________________________

3. A house protects us from ______________, ______________, ______________ and animals.

4. Two houses which can easily be shifted from one place to another.

   __________________________ and __________________________

5. Two natural things used to make houses.

   __________________________ and __________________________

6. Two types of roofs that are made depending upon the location of house.

   __________________________ and __________________________

Clothing

We wear clothes to protect us from cold, heat, rain and wind. Clothes also make us look smart and attractive. We wear different types of clothes according to the weather and occasions. We also wear accessories to match our outfits such as watch, bracelet, necklace, etc.

A. Can you identify the picture clues and write the types of clothes from the help box under them?

1. Why do we need clothes?

____

2. Name two different fibres used for making clothes.

____

3. Name two animals which give us fibres for making clothes.

____

4. Name two plants from which we obtain fibres for making clothes.

____

C. Complete the concept map given below.

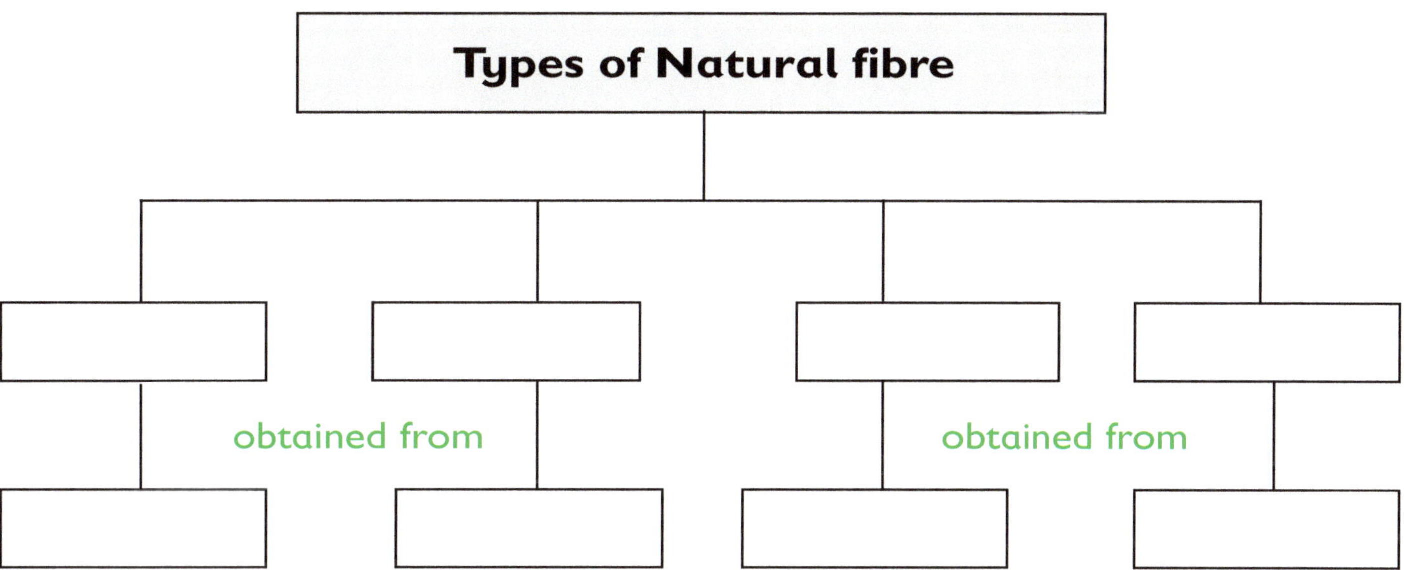

Air

Air is a mixture of different gases. Living things need air to stay alive and to prepare their food. We must breathe in clean air to keep ourselves healthy. Plants keep the air fresh and clean. Moving air is called wind which is used to generate electricity by humans.

A. Match the following.

Column I	Column II
Moving air is called	move
Gentle wind is called	wind
Air causes things to	dust
Air contains	storm
Strong wind is called	breeze

B. Fill in the blanks with the correct option.

1. We should ____________ trees to keep the air clean. (plant/cut)

2. Air gives ____________ to a balloon. (money/shape)

3. A ____________ can damage our houses and trees. (breeze/storm)

4. We must breathe in ____________ air. (fresh/polluted)

5. Air has ____________. (colours/weight)

C. Answer the questions given below.

1. Why do plants need air?

____

2. Why do animals need air?

____

3. How are plants helpful for us?

____

4. Name three objects in which air can be filled.

____

5. Name three things which need air to move.

____

D. Complete the concept map given below.

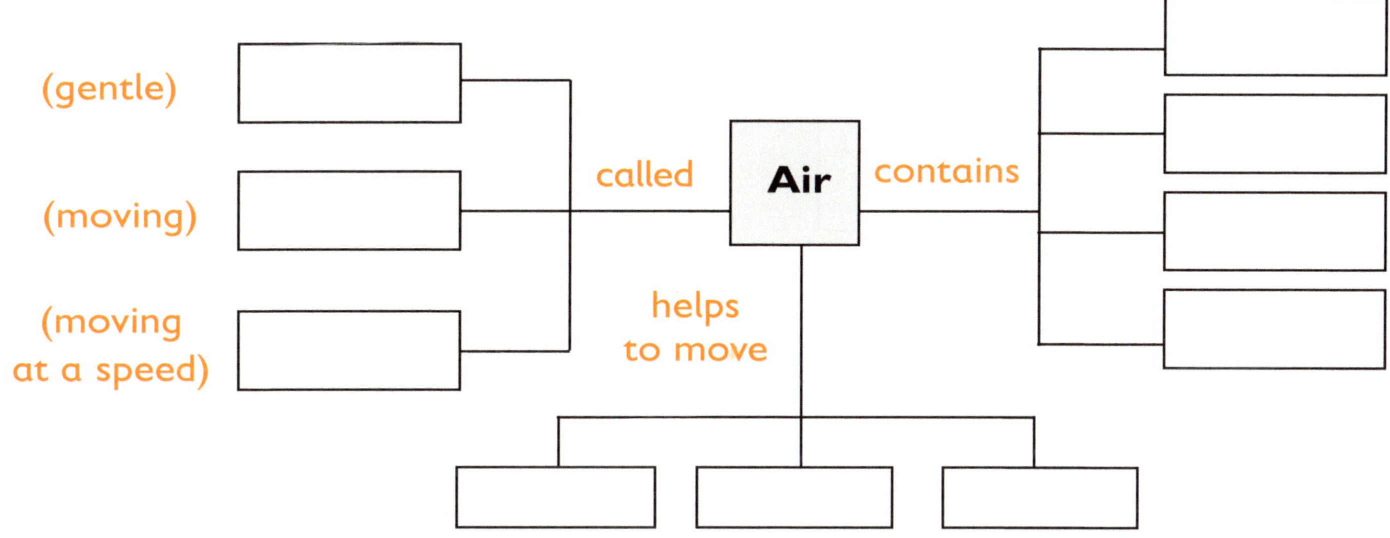

Water

Water is a clear liquid which is very important for all the living things to stay alive. It is a colourless and tasteless liquid. Water is available on Earth in large oceans but it is mostly salty. There are very few sources of fresh water which can be used by us.

A. Look at the word search given below. Find the names of 8 sources of water and write them in the given space.

P	W	Q	T	A	R	U	X	S	C
R	E	N	G	D	A	M	Q	W	A
V	L	C	O	D	I	Y	O	A	N
F	L	A	K	E	N	B	C	Z	A
H	J	T	R	R	I	V	E	R	L
L	W	Q	R	D	S	W	A	R	N
S	T	R	E	A	M	I	N	T	S

1. ________________ 2. ________________ 3. ________________ 4. ________________

5. ________________ 6. ________________ 7. ________________ 8. ________________

B. Write T for true statements and F for the false ones.

1. We should waste water while bathing.

2. Boiling water kills the germs.

3. We should store clean water in closed containers.

4. Drinking dirty water is a healthy habit.

5. We should never collect the rain water.

6. We get rain water from under the ground.

C. Answer the following questions.

1. What is rainwater?

   ____

2. What is groundwater?

   ____

3. Name three containers you can use to store water.

   ____

4. What does dirty water contain?

   ____

5. Name three places where rainwater flows into.

   ____

6. From where do you get water at your home?

   ____

D. Name two objects which:

1. Float in water.

2. Sink in water.

3. Dissolve in water.

4. Do not dissolve in water.

5. Add colour to water.

E. Fill in the blanks with the correct word.

1. Dirty water contains ______________. (germs/tap)

2. ____________ flows in ponds and lakes. (Rainwater/Tapwater)

3. We use a ___________ to store water in our homes. (tank/river)

4. We __________ water to kill the germs in it. (buy/boil)

5. Groundwater can be used by digging a ____________. (compost/well)

6. We should not _________ water. (use/waste)

F. Draw two containers in which you store clean water at your home.

G. Complete the concept maps below using the given clues.

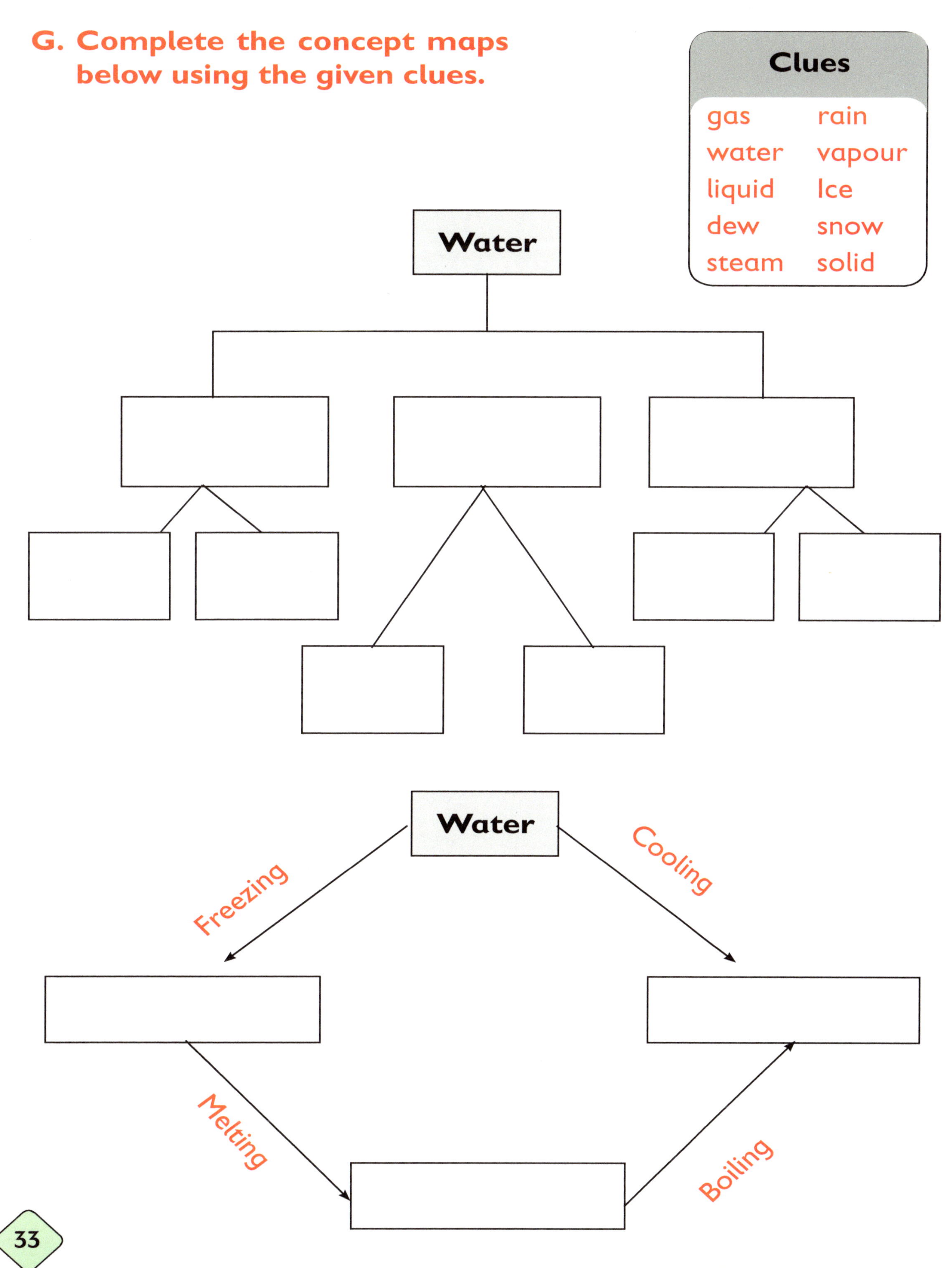

Day and Night

When the sun rises, its light and heat reach the surface of the Earth. It is called day time. When you cannot see the sun or its light from where you are, it is called night time. At any moment, half of the Earth has daytime and the other half has night time.

A. Look at the picture below. Discuss which part of Earth has daytime and which has nighttime and colour the picture.

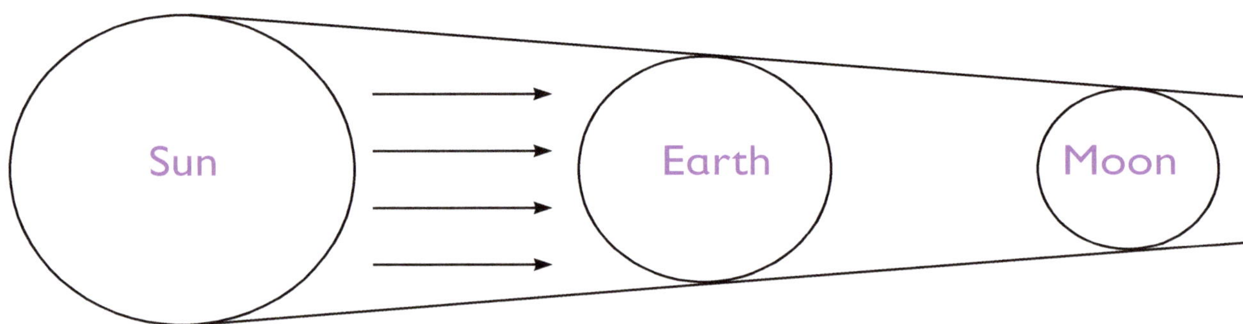

B. Give one word for the following.

1. Its movement causes day and night.

2. It gives us heat and light.

3. The time when sun is visible in the sky.

4. The time when light and heat from the sun can't reach you.

5. They twinkle in the sky at night.

6. It goes round the Earth. It shines at night and changes its shape.

C. Fill in the blanks given below.

1. It takes __________ hours to make one day and one night.

2. We cannot live on the Earth without the ____________.

3. Objects are visible only when there is __________.

4. To see objects clearly at night, we use __________ and __________.

5. The Earth ____________ on its axis. It causes day and night.

6. The sun rises from the ____________ and sets in the __________.

D. Answer the following questions.

1. What gives us light and heat?

   ____

2. What causes day and night?

   ____

3. What helps us to see objects around us?

   ____

4. Name two things you can see in the sky during the day.

   ____

5. Name two things you can see in the sky during the night.

   ____

Test Yourself 1

A. Fill in the blanks given below.

1. ________________ give us honey and wax.

2. Milk keeps our ________________ strong.

3. All the bones in our body together make the ________________.

4. ________________ are tall and strong plants.

5. ________________ and ________________ have weak stems.

6. ________________ is a solid form of water.

7. We should cross the road at a ________________.

8. ________________ is the biggest land animal in the world.

9. We get ________________ and ________________ from plants.

10. House protects us from ________________ and ________________.

B. Match the following.

Column I	Column II
Snail	Run
Bat	Swim
Penguin	Fly
Kangaroo	Crawl
Dolphin	Hop
Earthworm	Slither
Leopard	Glide
Bee	Slide

C. Name the following.

1. An animal which gives us wool. _______________

2. An animal which carries heavy loads for us. _______________

3. An animal which can live both on land and water. _______________

4. A plant with weak stem that spreads on ground. _______________

5. A plant which grows in deserts. _______________

6. It is bigger than the earth. _______________

7. It is smaller than the earth. _______________

8. A plant that grows in water. _______________

9. We fill this into a football. _______________

10. A place where two or more bones meet. _______________

D. The names of the water sources have jumbled up. Can you arrange them correctly?

1. MASTER _______________

2. LEAK _______________

3. PDON _______________

4. NAIR _______________

5. LIARGEC _______________

6. ABY _______________

7. LEWL _______________

8. ASE _______________

9. CONEA _______________

10. VIERR _______________

E. Name the animal or plant from where we get the following things.

1. Silk

2. Honey

3. Rubber

4. Milk

5. Wool

6. Wood

7. Paper

8. Cheese

9. Eggs

10. Spices

11. Cotton

12. Seeds

F. Write T for true statements and F for false ones.

1. Air contains dust and germs.

2. A lion lives in a stable.

3. Small plants with woody stem are called shrubs.

4. Fruits and vegetables are examples of protective foods.

5. There are 206 joints and over 300 bones in our body.

6. A house protects us from bad weather and wild animals.

7. A gentle wind is called a storm.

8. A house made from blocks of ice is called a hut.

G. Draw and name two objects for each of the following.

1. Summer clothes.

(a)	(b)

2. Things that need air to move.

(a)	(b)

3. Protective food items.

(a)	(b)

1. Why do we need a house?

   ____

2. Why should we follow safety rules?

   ____

3. Name the three meals we have in a day.

   ____

4. What is a skeleton?

   ____

5. Name three activities you can perform using your legs.

   ____

6. Name three activities you can perform using your hands.

   ____

Test Yourself 2

A. Fill in the blanks given below.

1. The ___________ gives shape and support to our body.

2. Water changes into _________ when it is boiled.

3. We use the ___________ by digging wells and hand pumps.

4. We must drink plenty of ___________ to remain healthy.

5. Our bones are covered with _______________.

6. Wild animals live in _______________.

7. _______________ is an example of a climber.

8. _______________ is an example of a creeper.

9. The strong and woody stem of a tree is called _______________.

10. ____________ gives us energy to work and play.

B. Give two examples for each of the following.

1. Energy-giving foods

2. Wild animals

3. Permanent houses

4. Temporary houses

5. Woollen clothes

6. Sources of light

7. Body-building foods

8. Domestic animals

C. Write one word for the following.

1. A gentle wind.

2. A strong wind that blows very fast.

3. Houses made of mud and straw.

4. A soft substance that covers the bones.

5. The meal that we have at night.

6. Places where two bones join together.

7. Animals that roam in the forests.

8.   It is formed when water freezes.

9.   It helps us to see things.

10. Plant which grows along the ground.

D. Write T for true statements and F for the false ones.

1.   Animals do not need water.

2.   Dirty water is good for our health.

3.   The Earth goes around the sun.

4.   A cat helps us move heavy loads.

5.   Bamboo tree has very weak stem.

6.   We should always keep a straight posture.

7.   We wear woollen clothes in summer season.

8.   A traffic light is of no use to us.

9.   We should eat as fast as we can.

10. We get jute and cotton fibres from plants.

E. Match the following.

Column I	Column II
Elephants live in	three different forms
Water can exist in	the Earth
Plants store their food	forests
The moon goes around	fight diseases
Fruits help us	breathing
We use air for	in the leaves

F. Answer the following.

1. Why do we need food?

   ____

2. Why do we need water and air?

   ____

3. How are plants useful for us?

   ____

4. What is a good posture?

   ____

5. What is a permanent house?

   ____

6. Why do we need clothes?

   ____

G. Draw and name two objects for each of the following.

1. Things in which you fill air:

(a)	(b)

2. Things we get from plants:

(a)	(b)

3. Things we get from animals:

(a)	(b)

Answers

Let's Revise

A. 1. Bee   2. Rabbit
   3. Spider   4. Eagle
   5. Horse   6. Cow
   7. Duck, Frog   8. Dog
   9. Bear   10. Lion

B. 1. F   2. T   3. T
   4. F   5. T   6. F

C. 1. herb   2. climber
   3. root   4. seed
   5. flower

D. 1. Eyes (see)   2. Ears (listen)
   3. Skin (feel)   4. Tongue (taste)
   5. Nose (smell)

E. 1. We need food to live.
   2. We need a house to stay safe from bad weather and wild animals.
   3. We wear clothes to cover our body and to look beautiful.

F. Bedroom, Bathroom

G. Raincoat, Gumboots

H. 1. Scarf   2. Shirt
   3. Socks   4. Shorts

Plants

B. 1. tree   2. Creepers
   3. Climbers   4. Herbs
   5. land, water   6. Shrubs

C. 1. Climbers and creepers have weak stem.
   2. Herbs are smaller and weaker than shrubs.
   3. Grapes plant, Pea plant, Bean plant.
   4. Trees have the longest life.
   5. Sunlight, air, water and soil.

D. 1. Cactus, Palm
   2. Lotus, Duckweed   3. Apple, Banana
   4. Onion, Potato   5. Tulip, Jasmine
   6. Banyan, Mint

E. 1. Jute plant   2. Cotton plant
   3. Mustard plant   4. Cinnamon tree

F. 1. Germination   2. Sapling
   3. Leaves   4. Flowers

G. Peanut, Papaya, Pulses, Peas, Paper, Pansy

H. Trees: Pine, Coconut
   Shrubs: Rose, Cotton plant
   Herbs: Mint, Spinach
   Climbers: Grapes, Pea plant
   Creepers: Pumpkin, Cucumber

World of Animals

A. Wild animals: Tiger, Leopard, Elephant, Vulture, Giraffe, Rhinoceros
   Domestic animals: Horse, Sheep, Goat, Camel, Bee, Duck

B. Sheep – Wool, Silkworm – Silk, Cow – Milk, Hen – Eggs, Bee – Honey

C. 1. Horse   2. Honey
   3. Duck   4. Silkworm
   5. Dog

D. 1. Goat, Deer, Rhinoceros
   2. Monkey, Lizard, Squirrel
   3. Eagle, Parrot, Owl
   4. Pigeon, Crow, Flamingo
   5. Snail, Tortoise,
   6. Lion, Horse
   7. Camel, Ox
   8. Zebra, Tiger
   9. Rabbit, Bear, Yak
   10. Bee, Wasp

E. 1. Lion
   2. Duck
   3. Crocodile
   4. Hyena

F. 1. Animals which are tamed by humans are domestic animals.
   2. Animals which live in the forest and cannot be tamed by humans are wild animals.
   3. Milk, wool and eggs.
   4. Forest, ocean, grassland
   5. Horse, donkey, camels, bulls

Our Body

A. 1. Eyes   2. Legs
   3. Hand   4. Nose
   5. Teeth   6. Knees
   7. Neck   8. Lips
   9. Ears   10. Foot

B. 1. bones, muscles   2. skeleton
   3. 206   4. joints
   5. exercise   6. posture

C. 1. T   2. F   3. T
   4. T   5. F   6. T
   7. T   8. F

Food for Health

A. Protective food: carrot, beans, apple, grapes, orange, spinach

Body-building food: milk, egg, pulses, meat, yogurt, tofu

Energy-giving food: wheat, banana, rice, oats, potatoes, nuts

B. 1. stale   2. hands
    3. energy   4. Body-building
    5. Wheat   6. water
    7. food   8. protective
C. 1. Energy-giving foods give us energy to do work.
    2. Body-building foods help our body to grow.
    3. A fixed event when people sit down to have their food.
    4. Protective foods protect us from diseases and keep us healthy.
    5. Eating meals at the right time ensures that our body gets energy at the right time.

Safety Rules

A. 1, 4, 6, 7
B. 1. Zebra crossing
    2. Swimming tube or air tube
    3. Traffic light
    4. Alarm
C. Fire, Nail

House

A. 1. Room   2. Roof
    3. Tent   4. Door
    5. Brick   6. Stone
    7. Flat   8. Hut
    9. Igloo   10. Cement
B. 1. ice   2. mud and straw
    3. cloth
C. Temporary houses: caravan, igloo, tent, teepee, hut, log cabin

Permanent houses: bungalow, apartment, cottage, castle, flat, mansion
E. 1. house
    2. animals and weather
    3. permanent
    4. temporary
    5. roofs
F. 1. Bricks and Cement
    2. Mud and Straw
    3. wind, weather, thieves
    4. Tent, Caravan
    5. Wood, Stones
    6. Flat and Slanting

Clothing

A. 1. Shirt   2. Raincoat
    3. Skirt   4. Cap
    5. Scarf   6. Socks
    7. Gloves   8. Boots
    9. Pants

B. 1. We need clothes to cover our body and to look pretty.
    2. Cotton, silk, jute
    3. Sheep and silkworm
    4. Cotton plant and jute plant
C. Cotton from cotton plant, Jute from jute plant
Silk from silkworm, Wool from sheep and yak

Air

A. 1. Moving air is called wind.
    2. Gentle wind is called breeze.
    3. Air causes things to move.
    4. Air contains dust.
    5. Strong wind is called storm.
B. 1. plant   2. shape
    3. storm   4. fresh
    5. weight
C. 1. Plants need air to make their food.
    2. Animals need air to stay alive.
    3. Plants clean the polluted air for us.
    4. Balloon, air tube, football, hot air balloon, hovercraft.
    5. Kite, birds, sail boat, windmill etc.
D. Called as: Breeze, wind, storm

Help to move: kite, hot air balloon, aeroplanes, birds

Contains: dust particles, gases, water vapours, germs

Water

A. Well, Stream, Lake, Dam, Rain, River, Canal, Ocean
B. 1. F   2. T   3. T
    4. F   5. F   6. F
C. 1. Water that we obtained through rain is called rainwater.
    2. Water stored under the ground in pores of soil and rocks is groundwater.
    3. Water tank, bottles, cans etc.
    4. Dirty water contains germs, dirt and chemicals.
    5. Rainwater flows into drains, rivers, dams and lakes.
    6. The water supply department of the state sends water through pipeline system.
D. 1. Wood log, Boat, Paper, Ball
    2. Stone, Metal spoon, Bicycle
    3. Salt, Sugar
    4. Pebbles, Paper, Dust
    5. Colour from flowers, Turmeric, Fruit juices
E. 1. germs   2. Rainwater
    3. tank   4. boil
    5. well   6. waste

Day and Night

B. 1. Earth 2. Sun
3. Day time 4. Night time
5. Stars 6. Moon

C. 1. 24 2. sun
3. light 4. lamp, torch
5. rotates 6. east, west

D. 1. Sun gives us heat and light.
2. The rotation of the Earth on its own axis causes day and night.
3. Light helps us to see objects around us.
4. Sun, clouds
5. Moon, stars

Test Yourself 1

A. 1. Bees 2. teeth
3. skeleton 4. Trees
5. Climbers, creepers 6. Ice
7. zebra crossing 8. Elephant
9. food, air 10. bad weather, animals

C. 1. Sheep 2. Donkey
3. Frog 4. Pumpkin
5. Cactus 6. Sun
7. Moon 8. Lotus
9. Air 10. Joint

D. 1. Stream 2. Lake
3. Pond 4. Rain
5. Glacier 6. Bay
7. Well 8. Sea
9. Ocean 10. River

E. 1. Silkworm 2. Bee
3. Rubber tree 4. Cow, Goat
5. Sheep, Yak 6. Tree
7. Tree 8. Cow, Goat
9. Hen, Duck 10. Plant
11. Cotton plant 12. Plants fruits

F. 1. T 2. F 3. T
4. T 5. F 6. T
7. F 8. F

H. 1. We need a house to stay inside and to protect ourselves from dangers.
2. We follow safety rules to stay safe.
3. Breakfast, lunch and dinner
4. Skeleton is the structure made by all the bones of our body.
5. Walk, kick, jump, run and hop.
6. Write, hold, push, pull and touch.

Test Yourself 2

A. 1. skeleton 2. steam
3. groundwater 4. water
5. muscles 6. forest
7. grapes 8. pumpkin
9. trunk 10. Energy-giving food

B. 1. Potato, Rice 2. Lion, Jaguar
3. Apartment, flat 4. Tent, hut
5. Coat, Sweater 6. Sun, Lamp
7. Milk, eggs 8. Horse, sheep

C. 1. Breeze 2. Storm
3. Hut 4. Muscles
5. Dinner 6. Joint
7. Wild animals 8. Ice
9. Light 10. Creepers

D. 1. F 2. F 3. T
4. F 5. F 6. T
7. F 8. F 9. F
10. T

F. 1. We need food to stay fit and healthy.
2. We need water and air to stay alive.
3. Plants provide us food and fresh air.
4. A good posture means to keep your back straight.
5. A permanent house is made up of bricks and cement and cannot be shifted to another place.
6. We need clothes to cover our body and to look beautiful.